JAN   2013

Multiplication and Division
SMARTS!

Lucille Caron
Philip M. St. Jacques

Enslow Publishers, Inc.
40 Industrial Road
Box 398
Berkeley Heights, NJ 07922
USA

http://www.enslow.com

Copyright © 2012 by Lucille Caron and Philip M. St. Jacques

Original edition published as *Multiplication and Division* in 2001.

Library of Congress Cataloging-in-Publication Data

Caron, Lucille.
  Multiplication and division smarts! / Lucille Caron and Philip M. St. Jacques.
      p. cm. — (Math smarts!)
  Summary: "Re-inforce classroom learning of important multiplication and
division skills including multiplication methods, and multiplying and dividing
time, money, and fractions"— Provided by publisher.
  Includes index.
  ISBN 978-0-7660-3937-7
  1. Multiplication—Juvenile literature. 2. Division—Juvenile literature.
  I. St. Jacques, Philip M. II. Title.
  QA115.C2424 2012
  513.2'13—dc22

                                                           2011008165

Paperback ISBN: 978-1-59845-320-1

Printed in China

052011 Leo Paper Group, Heshan City, Guangdong, China.

10 9 8 7 6 5 4 3 2 1

Cover Illustration: Shutterstock.com

Contents

Introduction 5

Multiplication

1 Multiplication and Repeated Addition 6

2 Multiplication Facts 8

3 Multiplying by Multiples of Ten 10

4 Multiplying With Regrouping 12

5 Multiplying Greater Numbers 14

6 Multiplication and Estimation 16

7 Multiplication Methods 18

8 Multiplication Properties 20

9 Multiplying Time 22

10 Multiplying Decimals 24

11 Multiplying Money 26

12 Multiplying Fractions 28

13 Multiplying Integers 30

Division

14 Division Facts 32

15 Multiplication and Division 34

16 More About Multiplication and Division 36

17 Dividing by Multiples of Ten 38

18 Dividing With Remainders 40

19 Dividing Greater Numbers 42

20 Division and Estimation 44

21 Division Properties 46

22 Division and Problem Solving... 48

23 Dividing Fractions 50

24 Dividing Mixed Numbers.. 52

25 Dividing Time 54

26 Dividing Decimals.. 56

27 Dividing Money.. 58

28 Dividing Integers.. 60

Further Reading and Internet Addresses 62

Index 63

Introduction

If you were to look up the meaning of the word *mathematics*, you would find that it is the study of numbers, quantities, and shapes, and how they relate to each other.

Mathematics is important to all world cultures, including our world of work. The following are just some of the ways in which studying math will help you:

▶ You will know how much money you are spending at the store.

▶ You will know if the cashier has given you the right change.

▶ You will know how to use measurements to build things.

▶ Your science classes will be easier and more interesting.

▶ You will understand music on a whole new level.

▶ You will be empowered to qualify for and land a rewarding job.

Multiplication and division are used in many professions and everyday activities—from figuring out prices per pound in the grocery store and calculating interest earned in bank accounts to buying enough material for construction jobs.

This book about multiplication and division has been written so that you can read it on your own, or with a friend, tutor, or parent.

Good luck and have fun!

Multiplication simplifies addition. You can think of multiplication as adding the same number again and again. For example, when you add 4 + 4, you have 2 fours, or 2×4.

Adding 3 sevens, 7 + 7 + 7, is the same as multiplying 3×7.

The symbol $\times$ is called the times sign and it means "multiplied by."

A shop sold a box of toy cars that had 3 rows with 5 cars in each row. How many cars were in the box?

Think of 3 groups of 5:

You can solve using repeated addition: 5 + 5 + 5, or you can rewrite 5 + 5 + 5 as 3 fives, or 3×5.

The first number (3) tells the number of rows.

The second number (5) tells how many cars are in each row.

The answer (15) is the total number of cars in the box.

Number Sentences

The above problem can be written as a number sentence:

$$3 \times 5 = 15.$$

This number sentence or multiplication equation can be read, "Three groups of five is 15."

The number sentence $3 \times 5 = 15$ is also called a **multiplication equation**.

Pictures can help you solve problems. They can help you see whether you are thinking correctly.

A painter is hired to paint all the houses on two blocks. Each block has three houses. How many houses will he paint?

block 1

block 2

In this problem there are two rows of houses. Each row represents one block. Each block has three houses. To find the total number of houses to be painted, add:

$$3 + 3 = 6, \qquad \text{or multiply 2 groups of 3:} \qquad 2 \times 3 = 6.$$

The numbers being multiplied are called factors. The answer is called the product.

Find the product of 4 × 5 using symbols.

Step 1: Draw 4 groups of 5.
Use any symbol you wish.

# # # # #
# # # # #
# # # # #
# # # # #

Step 2: Add all the symbols.

$$\begin{array}{r} \text{\# \# \# \# \#} = 5 \\ \text{\# \# \# \# \#} = 5 \\ \text{\# \# \# \# \#} = 5 \\ \text{\# \# \# \# \#} = +5 \\ \hline 20 \end{array}$$

The product of 4 × 5 is 20.

How many examples can you make in one minute using repeated addition and multiplication?

For example: $4 + 4 = 8$ is the same as $2 \times 4 = 8$.

factors — The numbers being multiplied.
product — The answer in a multiplication problem.

The basic multiplication facts are all the combinations of the numbers 0 through 9 multiplied by each other.

Multiplication Table

X	0	1	2	3	4	5	6	7	8	9
0	0	0	0	0	0	0	0	0	0	0
1	0	1	2	3	4	5	6	7	8	9
2	0	2	4	6	8	10	12	14	16	18
3	0	3	6	9	12	15	18	21	24	27
4	0	4	8	12	16	(20)	24	28	32	36
5	0	5	10	15	(20)	25	30	35	40	45
6	0	6	12	18	24	30	36	42	48	54
7	0	7	14	21	28	35	42	49	56	63
8	0	8	16	24	32	40	48	56	64	72
9	0	9	18	27	36	45	54	63	72	81

Each row has all the multiples of one-digit numbers. For example, the above marked row has all the multiples of 4. They were obtained by multiplying the numbers 0, 1, 2, 3, 4, 5, 6, 7, 8, and 9 by the number 4.

$4 \times 0 = 0$	$4 \times 1 = 4$	$4 \times 2 = 8$	$4 \times 3 = 12$	$4 \times 4 = 16$
$4 \times 5 = 20$	$4 \times 6 = 24$	$4 \times 7 = 28$	$4 \times 8 = 32$	$4 \times 9 = 36$

There are 100 basic multiplication facts. If you can memorize 55 of them, you'll know the other 45. Find 4×5 and 5×4 on the table (circled). The product of 4×5 and 5×4 is 20. If you know that $8 \times 7 = 56$, then you'll know that $7 \times 8 = 56$.

multiple — Any number multiplied by a counting number. For example, multiples of 3 are:

3, 6, 9, 12. . . .
(3×1) (3×2) (3×3) (3×4). . . .

Multiplying by Zero and by One

What is the product of 0 times any number?
Look at the table on page 8.

$3 \times 0 - 0$ $5 \times 0 - 0$ $7 \times 0 - 0$ $9 \times 0 - 0$

Any number times 0 is always 0.

What is the product of 1 times any number?

$2 \times 1 = 2$ $4 \times 1 = 4$ $6 \times 1 = 6$ $8 \times 1 = 8$

Any number times 1 is that number.

Other Basic Facts

Here is a list of some of the pairs of multiplication facts:

Twos
$2 \times 7 = 14$ and $7 \times 2 = 14$ $2 \times 2 = 4$

Threes
$3 \times 8 = 24$ and $8 \times 3 = 24$ $3 \times 3 = 9$

Fours
$4 \times 9 = 36$ and $9 \times 4 = 36$ $4 \times 4 = 16$

Fives
$5 \times 8 = 40$ and $8 \times 5 = 40$ $5 \times 5 = 25$

Sixes
$6 \times 9 = 54$ and $9 \times 6 = 54$ $6 \times 6 = 36$

Sevens
$7 \times 6 = 42$ and $6 \times 7 = 42$ $7 \times 7 = 49$

Eights
$8 \times 9 = 72$ and $9 \times 8 = 72$ $8 \times 8 = 64$

Nines
$9 \times 7 = 63$ and $7 \times 9 = 63$ $9 \times 9 = 81$

These pairs will make remembering multiplication facts easier.

Try memorizing the basic facts using multiplication pairs.

Any number times 0 is always 0.
Any number times 1 is always that number.

Multiplying by multiples of ten is a snap once you know the basic facts of multiplication. Consider multiplying 2×10.

The basic multiplication fact for this problem is the same as

$$2 \times 1.$$

The only difference is the zero in the number 10. The product of 2×1 is 2. Since 10 has one zero, place one zero to the right of the product. The answer is 20.

Multiplying by 10

Multiply 4×30

Step 1: Drop the zero and rewrite part of the example as a basic fact. 4×3

Step 2: Multiply the basic fact. $4 \times 3 = 12$

Step 3: Replace the zero and place one zero after the 12. $4 \times 30 = 120$

Multiplying by 100

Multiply 8×900

Step 1: Drop the zeros. Rewrite part of the example as a basic fact. 8×9

Step 2: Multiply the basic fact. $8 \times 9 = 72$

Step 3: Replace the zeros and place two zeros after the 72. $8 \times 900 = 7200$

To multiply a whole number by one hundred, multiply the basic fact and write two zeros to the right of the answer.

Multiplying by 1,000

Multiply 7 × 7,000

Step 1: Remove the zeros.   7 × 7

Step 2: Multiply the basic fact.   7 × 7 = 49

Step 3: Replace the zeros and place
three zeros after 49.   7 × 7,000 = 49,000

Multiplying by 10,000

Multiply 9 × 40,000

Step 1: Remove the zeros.   9 × 4

Step 2: Multiply the basic fact.   9 × 4 = 36

Step 3: Replace the zeros and
place four zeros after 36.   9 × 40,000 = 360,000

If you know the basic facts, it is easy to multiply by powers of ten.

If you earned $100,000 a month, would you be a millionaire at the end of one year? To multiply a whole number by one hundred thousand, multiply the basic fact and write five zeros to the right of the answer.

For multiplying or dividing by powers of ten, *see* the chart on page 39.

Multiplying With Regrouping

Your best friend gave you 3 boxes of baseball cards. Each box had 487 baseball cards. How many cards did you receive from your best friend? Use repeated addition to add the numbers.

$$487 + 487 + 487 = 1,461$$

Place Value

You can also multiply 3×487 using place value. Place value is another way to show three groups of 487.

The number 487 means 4 hundreds, 8 tens, and 7 ones.

Step 1: Multiply 3 by the value of each digit.

$3 \times 7 \text{ ones} = 3 \times 7 = 21$
$3 \times 8 \text{ tens} = 3 \times 80 = 240$
$3 \times 4 \text{ hundreds} = 3 \times 400 = 1,200$

Step 2: Add the products.

$21 + 240 + 1,200 = 1,461$

Regrouping

A third way to multiply 3×487 is to use regrouping.

Step 1: Multiply ones. $3 \times 7 \text{ ones} = 21$. Regroup. $21 = 2 \text{ tens and } 1 \text{ one}$. Write 1 in the ones place. Regroup 2 tens above the 8 in the tens place.

$$\begin{array}{r} \overset{2}{487} \\ \times\ 3 \\ \hline 1 \end{array}$$

Step 2: Multiply tens. $3 \times 8 \text{ tens} = 24 \text{ tens}$. Add 2 tens. $24 \text{ tens} + 2 \text{ tens} = 26 \text{ tens}$. Regroup. $26 \text{ tens} = 2 \text{ hundreds } 6 \text{ tens}$. Write 6 in the tens place. Regroup 2 hundreds above the 4 in the hundreds place.

$$\begin{array}{r} \overset{2\,2}{487} \\ \times\ 3 \\ \hline 61 \end{array}$$

There are often many different ways to find the answer to a math problem. Pick the method that you like the best and it will be easier for you to do it next time.

Step 3: Multiply hundreds.

$$3 \times 4 \text{ hundreds} = 12 \text{ hundreds. Add}$$
2 hundreds. 12 hundreds + 2 hundreds =
14 hundreds, or 1 thousand, 4 hundreds.

$$\begin{array}{r} 2\,2 \\ 487 \\ \times\ 3 \\ \hline 1461 \end{array}$$

Your friend gave you 1,461 baseball cards.

Using Partial Products

Multiply 68 × 29 using partial products.

Step 1: Multiply 68 by the ones digit of
the second number, 9. Regroup.
The answer is a partial product.

$$\begin{array}{r} 7 \\ 68 \\ \times\ 9 \\ \hline 612 \end{array}$$ **multiplicand**
multiplier
partial product

Step 2: Multiply 68 by the tens digit of the second number, 20.
Since 0 × 68 is zero, place a zero in the ones place.
Multiply 68 by 2 and place the answer in the tens column.

$$\begin{array}{r} 1 \\ 68 \\ \times\ 20 \\ \hline 1360 \end{array}$$

Step 3: Add the partial products. $1{,}360 + 612 = 1{,}972$

Checking the Answer

You can check your answer to a multiplication problem by switching the factors. Check your answer for the example above. When you multiplied 68 × 29, the product was 1,972. Check if the product is correct.

Step 1: Switch the factors (29 × 68). Multiply 29 by the ones digit of
the second factor, 8.

$$\begin{array}{r} 7 \\ 29 \\ \times\ 8 \\ \hline 232 \end{array}$$

Step 2: Multiply 29 by the tens digit of the second number, 60.
Place a zero in the ones place.

$$\begin{array}{r} 5 \\ 29 \\ \times\ 60 \\ \hline 1740 \end{array}$$

Step 3: Add the partial products. $1{,}740 + 232 = 1{,}972$

If the product is the same, your original answer is probably correct.

partial product — The product you get when you multiply by one digit at a time.

Suppose you have 127 compact discs. Each CD has 12 songs on it. How many songs are in your music collection? To find how many songs you have, multiply 127 by 12.

Step 1: Multiply by ones. $2 \times 7 = 14$. Write the 4 in the ones column and regroup the 1 to the tens column. Multiply 2×2 tens $= 4$ tens. Add 1 ten. 4 tens $+$ 1 ten $= 5$ tens. Write the 5 in the tens column. Multiply 2×1 hundred $= 2$ hundreds. Write 2 in the hundreds column.

$$\begin{array}{r} \overset{1}{127} \\ \times\ 12 \\ \hline 254 \end{array}$$

Step 2: Multiply by tens. $1 \times 7 = 7$. Write the 7 in the tens column underneath the 5. Multiply. $1 \times 2 = 2$. Write the 2 in the hundreds column underneath the 2. Multiply. $1 \times 1 = 1$. Write the 1 in the thousands column.

$$\begin{array}{r} 127 \\ \times\ 12 \\ \hline 254 \\ +\ 127 \\ \hline 1524 \end{array}$$

Step 3: Add the 2 rows of columns.

You have 1,524 songs in your music collection.

Have a family member write a three-digit-by-three-digit multiplication problem. Solve the problem on paper, then check your answer using a calculator.

Place Value

Name the place value of each digit in 234,957.

Digit	Value	Position	Words
2	200,000	hundred thousands	two hundred thousand
3	30,000	ten thousands	thirty thousand
4	4,000	thousands	four thousand
9	900	hundreds	nine hundred
5	50	tens	fifty
7	7	ones	seven

The number 234,957 is read "Two hundred thirty-four thousand nine hundred fifty-seven."

Multiplying Numbers That Have Zeros

You know that when any number is multiplied by zero, the answer is zero. What happens when you multiply numbers that have zeros in both factors?

Multiply 302 × 150.

Step 1: Since 0 × 302 = 0, place a zero in the ones column.

$$\begin{array}{r} 302 \\ \times\, 150 \\ \hline \mathbf{0} \end{array}$$

Step 2: Multiply the tens. When you multiply by 5, place the first digit in the tens column. 5 × 302 = 1510.

$$\begin{array}{r} 302 \\ \times\, 150 \\ \hline \mathbf{15100} \end{array}$$

Step 3: Multiply the hundreds. Place the first digit in the hundreds place. 1 × 302 = 302.

Step 4: Add.

$$\begin{array}{r} 302 \\ \times\, 150 \\ \hline 15100 \\ +\ \mathbf{302} \\ \hline \mathbf{45,300} \end{array}$$

Any number multiplied by zero is zero.

Estimation can be used to help you find out whether your answer to a math problem makes sense. You can first make an estimate of what you think the answer may be. Then you can find the exact answer. If the exact answer is close to your estimate, you can be more certain that your exact answer is correct.

Rounding to the Nearest Tens

To round a digit to the nearest tens, look at the ones digit.

For example, look at 4**8**.

If the ones digit is a 5, 6, 7, 8, or 9, add 1 to the digit in the tens place and replace all the digits to the right of the tens digit with zeros.

4**8** rounds to 50

If the ones digit is a 0, 1, 2, 3, or 4, the tens digit remains the same and all the digits to the right of it are replaced with a zero. For example, 4**4** rounds to 40.

Suppose your sports team had to sell candy to raise money for new uniforms. If there are 78 players and each player sold 6 boxes, about how many boxes were sold?

Step 1: Round 78 to the nearest tens. Since you have 8 ones, add one to the tens place and replace the digits to the right of the tens place with zeros.

$$\begin{array}{r} 7 \text{ tens } 8 \text{ ones} \\ + \text{ 1 ten} \\ \hline 8 \text{ tens } = 80 \end{array}$$

Step 2: Multiply the rounded number.

Approximately 480 boxes were sold by the team.

$$\begin{array}{r} 80 \\ \times\ 6 \\ \hline 480 \end{array}$$

estimation — An opinion or judgment; a best guess.

Round to the Nearest Hundreds

If you round 78 to the nearest hundreds, would you obtain a better estimate?

Estimate 6 × 78 by rounding 78 to the nearest hundreds.

Step 1: Look at the number in the tens column.

<u>7</u>8

If that number is 5 or higher, round up the number in the hundreds column by one.

78 = 0 hundreds, 7 tens, 8 ones

Rounding up one place in the hundreds column gives you:

1 hundred.

Step 2: Replace all the numbers to the right of the hundreds with zeros.

78 rounds to 100.

Step 3: Multiply the rounded number by the number of boxes of candy each player sold.

$100 \times 6 = 600$

According to this estimate, the players sold approximately 600 boxes of candy.

Exact vs. Estimate

Find the exact product of 6 × 78.

Step 1: Multiply ones. Regroup.

Step 2: Multiply tens.

$$\begin{array}{r} \overset{4}{7}8 \\ \times\ 6 \\ \hline 468 \end{array}$$

Compare the three products.

Rounding to tens	Exact	Rounding to hundreds
480	468	600

Rounding to the nearest tens gives you an answer closer to the exact product.

If you round to the smaller place value, the product will be closer to the exact answer. If you round to the greatest place value, the estimated product will be much farther from the exact answer.

Multiplication Methods

Students across the continents multiply in many different ways. Two different ways used to multiply whole numbers are the Russian peasant method and lattice multiplication.

Russian Peasant Method of Multiplication

Multiply 156 × 79 using the Russian peasant method.

Place one factor (156) in the first column and the other factor (79) in the second column. Take doubles of one factor and halves of the other factor. Double 156: 2 × 156 = 312. One half of 79 is 39.5. Drop the remainder. Keep doubling and halving until a 1 is reached in the halves column.

Doubles	Halves
156	79
312	39
624	19
1,248	9
2,496	4
4,992	2
+ 9,984	1
12,324	

Cross out all the even halves with their corresponding doubles. Then add the doubles column to find the product. The sum is 12,324. The product of 156 × 79 is 12,324.

That's cool.

Research different ways to multiply whole numbers.
How many ways did you find?

Lattice Multiplication

Another method used to multiply whole numbers is called lattice multiplication. Let's multiply 53 × 78 using lattice multiplication. A lattice is a series of squares with a diagonal drawn through it. Draw a lattice and place 53 along the top and 78 outside the right column.

Multiply each digit along the top by the digit along the right side. For example, 5 × 7 = 35. Write 35 in the box underneath the 5. Multiply 3 × 7. Write 21 in the box underneath the 3. Then multiply 5 × 8 (40) and 3 × 8 (24).

Add the numbers in the lattice along the diagonals. The bottom right diagonal only has a 4 in it. Bring down the 4. Add the next diagonal: 1 + 2 + 0 = 3. Write 3 underneath the 0 along the bottom horizontal. Add the next diagonal: 2 + 5 + 4 = 11. Write 1 along the left column alongside the 4. Regroup the other 1 to the next diagonal. Add the regrouped 1 + 3. Write the answer, 4, along the left column alongside the 3.

Read the product starting on the left column. The product of 53 × 78 is 4,134.

If one method — traditional, Russian peasant, or lattice — is easiest for you, use it!

There are six multiplication properties:

1. **Closure Property**
2. **Commutative Property**
3. **Associative Property**

4. **Property of One**
5. **Zero Property**
6. **Distributive Property**

Closure Property

If you multiply any two whole numbers, the product is always a whole number.

Example: 7 × 6 = 42

Commutative Property

The product of 3 × 4 will be the same as the product of 4 × 3.
The product of 3 × 4 = 12. The product of 4 × 3 = 12.
Therefore, 3 × 4 = 4 × 3.

Associative Property

If you multiply three or more numbers, the order in which you multiply them does not affect the answer.

Example: 4 × 2 × 3

You can only multiply two numbers at a time. Group two numbers using parentheses.

$$(4 \times 2) \times 3$$
$$8 \quad \times 3 = 24$$

Group the three numbers in a different way:

$$4 \times (2 \times 3)$$
$$4 \times \quad 6 = 24$$

As you can see, (4 × 2) × 3 = 4 × (2 × 3).

When you multiply numbers, the order is not important.

Property of One

The product of one and any number is that same number.

Examples:

$$4 \times 1 = 4$$
$$1 \times 6 = 6$$
$$8 \times 1 = 8$$

Zero Property

The product of zero and any number is always zero.

Examples:

$$2 \times 0 = 0$$
$$0 \times 3 = 0$$
$$5 \times 0 = 0$$

Distributive Property of Multiplication Over Addition

Example: $8 \times (6 + 5) = (8 \times 6) + (8 \times 5)$

Solve: $8 \times (6 + 5)$

Add.	$6 + 5 = 11$
Multiply.	$8 \times 11 = \mathbf{88}$

Solve: $(8 \times 6) + (8 \times 5)$

Multiply.	$8 \times 6 = 48 \qquad 8 \times 5 = 40$
Add.	$48 + 40 = \mathbf{88}$

You get the same answer either way.

With a friend play property concentration. Write the properties (such as *zero property*) on some cards and examples of the properties (such as *9 × 0*) on other cards. Mix them up, spread them face down, and take turns to find pairs. Whoever makes the most matches wins.

Parentheses mean "Do me first!"

How many hours a day are you in school? How many hours a day do you sleep? Watch television? How many hours do you do each activity in a week? How long is this in minutes?

Units of Time

The list below shows the relationship between different units of time:

60 seconds = 1 minute   60 minutes = 1 hour
24 hours = 1 day   7 days = 1 week
52 weeks = 1 year   12 months = 1 year
365 days = 1 year   366 days = 1 leap year
10 years = 1 decade   100 years = 1 century
1,000 years = 1 millennium

Changing Weeks to Hours

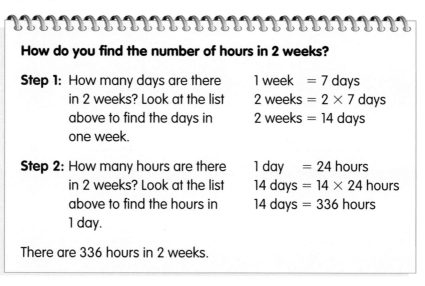

How do you find the number of hours in 2 weeks?

Step 1: How many days are there in 2 weeks? Look at the list above to find the days in one week.

1 week = 7 days
2 weeks = 2 × 7 days
2 weeks = 14 days

Step 2: How many hours are there in 2 weeks? Look at the list above to find the hours in 1 day.

1 day   = 24 hours
14 days = 14 × 24 hours
14 days = 336 hours

There are 336 hours in 2 weeks.

24 hours = 1 day
60 seconds = 1 minute

Changing Weeks to Minutes

How many minutes are there in 2 weeks?

From the last question, you know there are 336 hours in 2 weeks. There are 60 minutes in an hour.

To find the number of minutes in 2 weeks, multiply 336 hours by 60 minutes.

Step 1: Multiply by ones. When any number is multiplied by zero, the product is zero: $0 \times 366 = 0$. Place the zero in the units column.

$$\begin{array}{r} 336 \\ \times\ 60 \\ \hline 0 \end{array}$$

Step 2: Multiply by tens. Regroup.

There are 20,160 minutes in 2 weeks.

$$\begin{array}{r} 23 \\ 336 \\ \times\ 60 \\ \hline 20{,}160 \end{array}$$

Changing Days to Hours

How many hours are there in $3\frac{1}{2}$ days?

24 hours = 1 day

24 hours $\times$ 3 days = 72 hours (in 3 days)

$24 \times \frac{1}{2}$ = 12 hours (in half a day)

$72 + 12$ = 84 hours (in $3\frac{1}{2}$ days)

Changing Years to Months

How many months are there in 4 years?

12 months = 1 year

12 months $\times$ 4 = 48 months (in 4 years)

Changing Weeks to Days

If your family takes a 3-week vacation, for how many days will you be gone?

7 days = 1 week

7 days $\times$ 3 = 21 days

Using the number **60** as a measurement of time was probably started by the ancient Babylonians.

Decimals are used to report batting averages. They are also used in unit pricing. The next time you are at the supermarket, look at the unit price of your favorite snack. Unit prices are used to compare the prices of items.

Multiplying a Decimal by a Whole Number

Decimals are often used in sporting events. Suppose you were training for the track team and you jogged 0.4 mile 6 times a week. How many miles would you jog in a week?

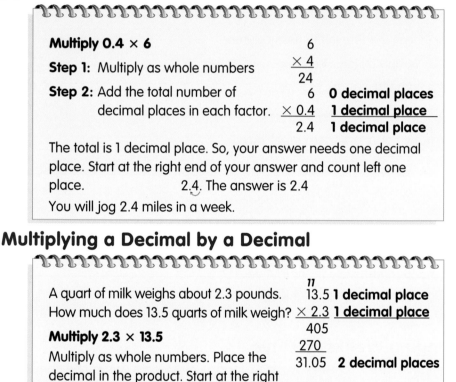

Multiply 0.4 × 6

Step 1: Multiply as whole numbers

$$\begin{array}{r} 6 \\ \times\,4 \\ \hline 24 \end{array}$$

Step 2: Add the total number of decimal places in each factor.

$$\begin{array}{r} 6 \quad \textbf{0 decimal places} \\ \times\,0.4 \quad \underline{\textbf{1 decimal place}} \\ \hline 2.4 \quad \textbf{1 decimal place} \end{array}$$

The total is 1 decimal place. So, your answer needs one decimal place. Start at the right end of your answer and count left one place.   2.4. The answer is 2.4

You will jog 2.4 miles in a week.

Multiplying a Decimal by a Decimal

A quart of milk weighs about 2.3 pounds. How much does 13.5 quarts of milk weigh?

$$\begin{array}{r} \overset{11}{13.5} \quad \textbf{1 decimal place} \\ \times\,2.3 \quad \textbf{1 decimal place} \\ \hline 405 \\ \underline{270} \\ 31.05 \quad \textbf{2 decimal places} \end{array}$$

Multiply 2.3 × 13.5

Multiply as whole numbers. Place the decimal in the product. Start at the right and move the decimal point two places to the left.

13.5 quarts of milk weighs 31.05 pounds.

The last thing you do when multiplying decimals is to place the decimal point in the answer.

Multiply 0.19 × 0.076

Multiply as whole numbers.

To place the decimal in the product, start at the right and move the point five places to the left.

$$
\begin{array}{r}
0.19 \quad \textbf{2 decimal places} \\
\times\ 0.076 \quad \textbf{3 decimal places} \\
\hline
114 \\
133 \\
\hline
0.01444 \quad \textbf{5 decimal places}
\end{array}
$$

In this problem it was necessary to write zeros in the answer to place the decimal point. You also write a zero before the decimal point. This zero serves as a placeholder.

Remember these steps when multiplying decimals:

1. Multiply the factors (numbers) the same way you multiply whole numbers.
2. Add the total number of decimal places in all factors.
3. Place the decimal point in the product. Start by counting from the right and move left the same number of places as the number of decimal places in the factors.
4. When necessary, write zeros in the product to place the decimal point.

Go shopping with a friend. Find the unit price for your favorite breakfast cereal. How much would 10 pounds of it cost?

One of the most popular reasons to multiply decimals is to figure out money: How much will you earn? How much will you spend? How many can you afford to buy?

Multiplying Money Amounts and Whole Numbers

How much would it cost to buy seven balls that cost $1.98 each?

Multiply 7 × $1.98

Multiply as whole numbers. Count the total of decimal places in each factor.

$$
\begin{array}{r}
6\,5 \\
1.98 \\
\times\quad 7 \\
\hline
1386
\end{array}
$$

2 decimal places
0 decimal places
2 decimal places

The answer will have the same number of decimal places as the total number of decimal places in both factors. Counting from right to left, place the decimal point in your answer.

$13.86 ← **start here and move two places to the left**

Place a dollar sign in the product. The cost of 7 balls at $1.98 each is $13.86.

Multiplying Money Amounts and Decimals

Your friend bought 0.5 yards of material for a costume. Each yard cost $2.75. How much did she pay for the material?

Multiply 0.5 × $2.75

Multiply as whole numbers. Counting from the right, place the decimal point in the product 3 places to the left.

$$
\begin{array}{r}
3\,2 \\
2.75 \\
\times\ 0.5 \\
\hline
1.375
\end{array}
$$

2 decimal places
1 decimal place
3 decimal places

Your friend paid $1.375. She could not give the cashier $1.375, so the number was rounded to the nearest cent: $1.38.

Rounding Money Amounts

The answer in the previous problem was $1.375. The 1 is in the ones place, the 3 is in the tenths place, the 7 is in the hundredths place, and the 5 is in the thousandths place.

ones	.	tenths	hundredths	thousandths
1	.	3	7	5

When there is a 5 or greater in the thousandths place, round up the hundredths place by one. If there is a 4 or less in the thousandths place, the hundredths place remains the same.

Examples: $1.375 $\longrightarrow$ $1.38

$3.152 $\longrightarrow$ $3.15

Multiplying Money Amounts By Powers of Tens

When multiplying a decimal by a power of ten, move the decimal point as many places to the right as there are zeros in the number you are multiplying by.

To multiply a decimal by	Move the decimal point
10	1 place to the right
100	2 places to the right
1,000	3 places to the right
10,000	4 places to the right

Suppose you wanted to purchase 1,000 pieces of gum at $0.160 each. What is the total cost?

Multiply $0.160 × 1000

$0.160 × 1,000 = $160.

Move the decimal point three places to the right.

You would pay $160 for 1,000 pieces of gum.

Use a merchandise catalog to find the cost of your favorite video. What would be the cost of 10 of these videos? 100? 1,000?

Can you think of a time when you divided items into halves, thirds, quarters, or eighths, such as cutting a pizza pie into eighths, sharing a candy bar, or making a family recipe?

Multiplying a Whole Number by a Fraction

Suppose a recipe calls for 3 cups of sugar and you and your friend want to make half the recipe. How many cups of sugar do you need?

Multiply $\frac{1}{2} \times 3$

Step 1: Write the whole number (3) as a fraction by placing it over 1.

$$\frac{1}{2} \times \frac{3}{1}$$

Step 2: Multiply the numerators. Multiply the denominators.

numerators
denominators
$$\frac{1 \times 3}{2 \times 1} = \frac{3}{2}$$

Step 3: Write the answer, an improper fraction, as a mixed number.

$$\frac{3}{2} = \frac{1}{2} + \frac{1}{2} + \frac{1}{2}$$

You need $1\frac{1}{2}$ cups of sugar.

$$\frac{3}{2} = 1\frac{1}{2}$$

Multiplying a Fraction by a Fraction

Suppose the same recipe calls for $\frac{1}{4}$ teaspoon of salt. How much salt do you need for half a recipe?

Multiply $\frac{1}{4} \times \frac{1}{2}$

Multiply the numerators.
Multiply the denominators.
You need $\frac{1}{8}$ teaspoon of salt.

$$\frac{1}{4} \times \frac{1}{2} = \frac{1 \times 1}{4 \times 2} = \frac{1}{8}$$

numerator — The number in the top of a fraction.
denominator — The number in the bottom of a fraction.
improper fraction — A fraction whose numerator is larger than its denominator.

Multiplying a Mixed Number by a Fraction

When dealing with real life situations, sometimes it is necessary to multiply mixed numbers. A mixed number contains a whole number and a fraction.

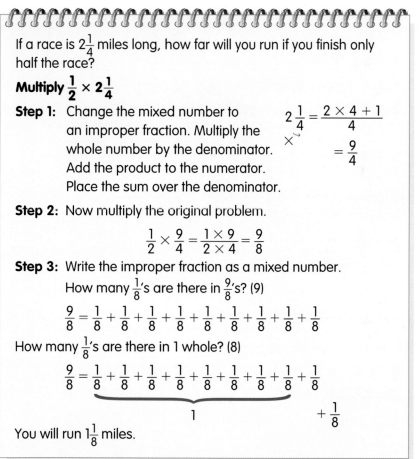

If a race is $2\frac{1}{4}$ miles long, how far will you run if you finish only half the race?

Multiply $\frac{1}{2} \times 2\frac{1}{4}$

Step 1: Change the mixed number to an improper fraction. Multiply the whole number by the denominator. Add the product to the numerator. Place the sum over the denominator.

$$2\frac{1}{4} = \frac{2 \times 4 + 1}{4}$$
$$= \frac{9}{4}$$

Step 2: Now multiply the original problem.

$$\frac{1}{2} \times \frac{9}{4} = \frac{1 \times 9}{2 \times 4} = \frac{9}{8}$$

Step 3: Write the improper fraction as a mixed number.

How many $\frac{1}{8}$'s are there in $\frac{9}{8}$'s? (9)

$$\frac{9}{8} = \frac{1}{8} + \frac{1}{8} + \frac{1}{8} + \frac{1}{8} + \frac{1}{8} + \frac{1}{8} + \frac{1}{8} + \frac{1}{8} + \frac{1}{8}$$

How many $\frac{1}{8}$'s are there in 1 whole? (8)

$$\frac{9}{8} = \underbrace{\frac{1}{8} + \frac{1}{8} + \frac{1}{8} + \frac{1}{8} + \frac{1}{8} + \frac{1}{8} + \frac{1}{8} + \frac{1}{8}}_{1} + \frac{1}{8}$$

You will run $1\frac{1}{8}$ miles.

One of your family members is making your favorite dish, but they only want to make half a recipe. Can you cut the entire recipe in half?

mixed number — A number that contains a whole number and a fraction.

Like integers are integers with the same sign. You can multiply two positive integers or two negative integers. You can also multiply unlike integers—one positive and one negative.

Multiplying Two Positive Integers

Multiply $^+9 \times {}^+7$

Step 1: Multiply as whole numbers. $9 \times 7 = 63$

Step 2: Place the sign. $^+9 \times {}^+7$ is the $^+9 \times {}^+7 = {}^+63$
same as 9×7. $9 \times 7 = 63$

Positive integers can be written with or without a positive sign.

Multiplying Two Negative Integers

Multiply $^-8 \times {}^-6$

Step 1: Multiply as whole numbers. $8 \times 6 = 48$

Step 2: Place the sign. The product of two $^-8 \times {}^-6 = 48$
negative integers is positive.

Multiplying Unlike Integers

Multiply $3 \times {}^-4$

Step 1: Multiply as whole numbers. $3 \times 4 = 12$

Step 2: Place the sign. The product $3 \times {}^-4 = {}^-12$
of one negative integer and
one positive integer is negative.

The product of two negative integers is **positive**. The product of one negative integer and one positive integer is **negative**.

Suppose you own some stock in a company. The stock has been going down for the last four days. Each day it has lost two points. How many points has your stock lost?

There are two ways to solve this problem.

1. Use repeated addition.

You can write a loss of two points as $^-2$, read as "negative two." The negative sign is placed either on the top left corner of the number or in the middle of the number ($^-2$). To figure out how many points the stock lost over four days, add $^-2$ four times.

Add:

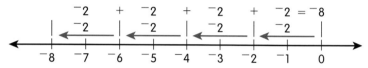

$$^-2 \; + \; ^-2 \; + \; ^-2 \; + \; ^-2 = \; ^-8$$

The stock lost eight points.

2. Use multiplication.

Multiply four days times $^-2$: $4 \times \; ^-2 = \; ^-8.$

Notice the 4 is a positive number, the 2 is a negative number, and the product is a negative number. When you multiply a positive number and a negative number, the product is negative.

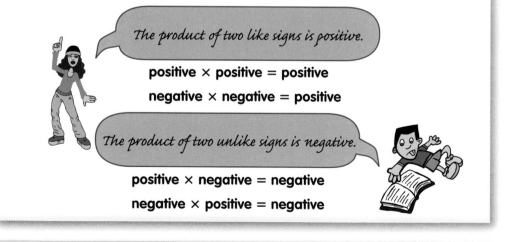

The product of two like signs is positive.

positive × positive = positive

negative × negative = positive

The product of two unlike signs is negative.

positive × negative = negative

negative × positive = negative

A **positive integer** is greater than zero and a **negative integer** is less than zero.

Suppose you had 16 tennis balls and you wanted to distribute them equally among your 8 friends. How many tennis balls will you give each friend?

How many groups of 8 tennis balls can you make from a group of 16 balls?

A group of 16 tennis balls can be separated into eight groups of two. You can write this as $16 \div 8 = 2$.

Basic Division Facts

Zero

Division by zero is impossible.

Example: $1 \div 0 = ?$

Rewrite this division sentence as a multiplication sentence:

$$0 \times ? = 1$$

This multiplication sentence is read, "zero times what whole number will give you one?" Since zero times any number is always zero, there is no whole number you can use to make this number sentence true. Therefore, division by zero cannot be done.

On the other hand, zero divided by any number is still zero:

$0 \div 1 = 0$	$0 \div 2 = 0$	$0 \div 3 = 0$
$0 \div 4 = 0$	$0 \div 5 = 0$	$0 \div 6 = 0$
$0 \div 7 = 0$	$0 \div 8 = 0$	$0 \div 9 = 0$

I can do this.

What two related **division facts** can you write for $6 \times 8 = 48$?

One
Any number divided by one is that number:

$0 \div 1 = 0$, $1 \div 1 = 1$, $2 \div 1 = 2$, $3 \div 1 = 3$, $4 \div 1 = 4$,
$5 \div 1 = 5$, $6 \div 1 = 6$, $7 \div 1 = 7$, $8 \div 1 = 8$, $9 \div 1 = 9$

Two
$2 \div 2 = 1$, $4 \div 2 = 2$, $6 \div 2 = 3$, $8 \div 2 = 4$, $10 \div 2 = 5$,
$12 \div 2 = 6$, $14 \div 2 = 7$, $16 \div 2 = 8$, $18 \div 2 = 9$

Three
$3 \div 3 = 1$, $6 \div 3 = 2$, $9 \div 3 = 3$, $12 \div 3 = 4$, $15 \div 3 = 5$,
$18 \div 3 = 6$, $21 \div 3 = 7$, $24 \div 3 = 8$, $27 \div 3 = 9$

Four
$4 \div 4 = 1$, $8 \div 4 = 2$, $12 \div 4 = 3$, $16 \div 4 = 4$, $20 \div 4 = 5$,
$24 \div 4 = 6$, $28 \div 4 = 7$, $32 \div 4 = 8$, $36 \div 4 = 9$

Five
$5 \div 5 = 1$, $10 \div 5 = 2$, $15 \div 5 = 3$, $20 \div 5 = 4$, $25 \div 5 = 5$,
$30 \div 5 = 6$, $35 \div 5 = 7$, $40 \div 5 = 8$, $45 \div 5 = 9$

Six
$6 \div 6 = 1$, $12 \div 6 = 2$, $18 \div 6 = 3$, $24 \div 6 = 4$, $30 \div 6 = 5$,
$36 \div 6 = 6$, $42 \div 6 = 7$, $48 \div 6 = 8$, $54 \div 6 = 9$

Seven
$7 \div 7 = 1$, $14 \div 7 = 2$, $21 \div 7 = 3$, $28 \div 7 = 4$, $35 \div 7 = 5$,
$42 \div 7 = 6$, $49 \div 7 = 7$, $56 \div 7 = 8$, $63 \div 7 = 9$

Eight
$8 \div 8 = 1$, $16 \div 8 = 2$, $24 \div 8 = 3$, $32 \div 8 = 4$, $40 \div 8 = 5$,
$48 \div 8 = 6$, $56 \div 8 = 7$, $64 \div 8 = 8$, $72 \div 8 = 9$

Nine
$9 \div 9 = 1$, $18 \div 9 = 2$, $27 \div 9 = 3$, $36 \div 9 = 4$, $45 \div 9 = 5$,
$54 \div 9 = 6$, $63 \div 9 = 7$, $72 \div 9 = 8$, $81 \div 9 = 9$

Memorize the division facts with a friend.

Multiplication and division are inverse operations. The inverse operation undoes what another operation does. It's like lacing and unlacing your shoes, buttoning and unbuttoning your coat, or turning a faucet on and off. What other operations are inverse operations? Subtraction is the inverse of addition:

addition	subtraction
$8 + 9 = 17$	$17 - 8 = 9$

Multiplying Whole Numbers

When two whole numbers are multiplied, the answer will be greater than either of the factors.

$$factor \times factor = product$$

For example: $3 \times 4 = 12$

• • • •
• • • •
• • • •

The product (12) is greater than either factor (3 or 4).

Dividing Whole Numbers

Dividing whole numbers results in a smaller number than the number being divided. Consider a group of 12 stars. How many groups of 3 stars can you make from a group of 12 stars?

A group of 12 stars can be separated into 4 groups of three.
Dividing 12 stars by 3 gives you an answer smaller than 12.

Whole numbers include all the counting numbers and zero:
0, 1, 2, 3, . . .

Basic Facts

Knowing the multiplication facts will help you solve division problems. In multiplication you put groups together. In division you take groups apart. So, when you divide, think of a related multiplication fact.

What is the missing number in the following example:

$$2 \times ? = 10$$

Use a number line to find the missing number.

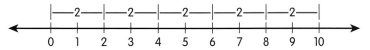

Begin at zero and mark off 2 units. Continue marking off groups of two units until you reach 10. Count the number of groups you marked off. The missing number is 5.

The multiplication equation $2 \times ? = 10$ can be written as a division equation.

$$10 \div 2 = ?$$

Since division is the inverse of multiplication, you can think of division in terms of finding a missing factor.

$$10 \div 2 = ? \text{ can be thought of as } 2 \times ? = 10$$

The basic multiplication facts related to this example are

$$2 \times 5 = 10 \text{ and } 5 \times 2 = 10$$

The basic division facts related to this example are

$$10 \div 2 = 5 \text{ and } 10 \div 5 = 2$$

Remember: In **multiplication** you put groups together.
In **division** you take groups apart. For more division facts, see pages 32–33.

Inverse Operation

Division is the inverse of multiplication. The basic facts of division are the opposites of the basic facts of multiplication.

Basic Multiplication Fact: $5 \times 6 = 30$ and $6 \times 5 = 30$

Basic Division Fact: $30 \div 5 = 6$ and $30 \div 6 = 5$

Since division is the inverse of multiplication, think of division in terms of multiplication by finding the missing factor.

Multiplication: factor $\times$ factor = product
Division: product $\div$ factor = factor
Example: $56 \div 7 = ?$ can be thought of as
$7 \times ? = 56$
$7 \times 8 = 56$, so $56 \div 7 = 8$

The missing factor is 8.

You can use multiples to find the missing factor.

multiples of 7: 7, 14, 21, 28, 35, 42, 49, 56

Finding the multiples is the same as counting by sevens.
How many sevens are there in 56? (8).

If you have studied and understand the multiplication table on page 8, division will be a snap.

inverse operations:
    Addition is the inverse of subtraction.
    Multiplication is the inverse of division.

Terms

Division has its own vocabulary. The following terms are used in division:

quotient   the answer

dividend   the number that you divide

divisor   the number by which you divide

Three symbols are used to indicate division:

1. $\overline{)}$ **long division** $\text{divisor}\overline{)\text{dividend}}^{\textbf{quotient}}$

2. —— **fraction bar** $\dfrac{\textbf{dividend}}{\textbf{divisor}} = \textbf{quotient}$

3. ÷   **division symbol**   **dividend ÷ divisor = quotient**

Here is a division problem written three ways:

$$\begin{array}{r} 4 \\ 9{\overline{)36}} \end{array} \qquad \frac{36}{9} = 4 \qquad 36 \div 9 = 4$$

They are read the same way: "Thirty-six divided by nine equals four."

You can also write the equation as a multiplication fact:

$$9 \times 4 = 36$$

$$36 \div 9 = 4 \text{ is the inverse of } 9 \times 4 = 36$$

Thirty-six divided into nine groups makes four in each group. Nine groups of four make a total of thirty-six.

36 is the **dividend** in the division equation and the **product** in the multiplication equation.

If you went to the bank to cash a $25,000 check and asked the teller for ten-dollar bills, how would you know if she gave you the right number of bills? How many ten-dollar bills are there in $25,000?

Dividing by Ten

When you divide by ten, you move the decimal point one place to the left. Let's look at the first question:

How many ten-dollar bills are there in $25,000?

Step 1: Write a division equation. $25,000 \div $10 = ?

Step 2: Place a decimal point after the money amount. $25,000. \div $10 = ?

Step 3: Move the decimal point one place to the left because you are dividing by 10, which has one zero. $25,000. \div $10 = 2500

There are 2,500 ten-dollar bills in $25,000.

Dividing by a Hundred

When you divide by 100, you move the decimal point two places to the left.

How many hundred-dollar bills are there in $25,000?

Step 1: Write a division equation. $25,000 \div $100 = ?

Step 2: Place a decimal point after the money amount. $25,000. \div $100 = ?

Step 3: Move the decimal point two places to the left, because 100 has two zeros. $25,000. \div $100 = 250

There are 250 hundred-dollar bills in $25,000.

All numbers that end in **zero** can be divided evenly by 10.

Summary of Multiplying and Dividing by Powers of Ten

When multiplying or dividing by multiples of 10, move the decimal point to the indicated position.

Power of Ten	Multiply	Divide
10	1 place to the right	1 place to the left
Example:	$65 \times 10 = 650$	$65 \div 10 = 6.5$
100	2 places to the right	2 places to the left
Example:	$65 \times 100 = 6{,}500$	$65 \div 100 = 0.65$
1,000	3 places to the right	3 places to the left
Example:	$65 \times 1{,}000 = 65{,}000$	$65 \div 1{,}000 = 0.065$
10,000	4 places to the right	4 places to the left
Example:	$65 \times 10{,}000 = 650{,}000$	$65 \div 10{,}000 = 0.0065$
100,000	5 places to the right	5 places to the left
Example:	$65 \times 100{,}000 = 6{,}500{,}000$	$65 \div 100{,}000 = 0.00065$

Multiplying by multiples of 10 produces a larger answer and dividing by multiples of 10 produces a smaller answer.

Use the table above to understand the following examples:

Multiply 56×10
Move the decimal one place to the right. $56 \times 10 = 560.$
$$56 \times 10 = 560$$

Divide $56 \div 10$
Move the decimal one place to the left. $56 \div 10 = 5.6$
$$56 \div 10 = 5.6$$

Notice that 560 is greater than 5.6.

Multiplying or dividing by a power of ten is as simple as moving the decimal point.

Suppose you took 103 photographs and you wanted to put 6 photographs on each page of your new album. How many pages will you fill? How many photographs will be on the last page?

Divide 103 ÷ 6

Step 1: Does 6 go into 1? (no)
Does 6 go into 10? (yes)
How many 6s are there in 10?
(1) Place the 1 over the 0.

$$\begin{array}{r} 1 \\ 6\overline{)103} \end{array}$$

Step 2: Multiply (1 × 6 = 6). Write the product below the 10. Then subtract (10 − 6 = 4). The difference must be less than the divisor (6).

$$\begin{array}{r} 1 \\ 6\overline{)103} \\ -\ 6 \\ \hline 4 \end{array}$$

Step 3: Bring down the next digit in the dividend (3). Divide. How many 6s are there in 43? (7) Place the 7 in the quotient above the 3. Multiply (7 × 6 = 42). Subtract (43 − 42 = 1).

$$\begin{array}{r} 17 \\ 6\overline{)103} \\ -\ 6\downarrow \\ \hline 43 \\ -\ 42 \\ \hline 1 \end{array}$$

Step 4: Write the remainder in the quotient.

$$\begin{array}{r} 17\,\text{R}1 \\ 6\overline{)103} \end{array}$$

You write the remainder (R) in the quotient. The answer is called the quotient and is read, "17 remainder 1." You will fill 17 pages, and 1 photograph will be on the eighteenth page.

The **remainder** is the number left over in a division problem.

The Largest Possible Remainder

What is the largest possible remainder any problem could have? Let's do the following problem to answer this question.

Divide 369 ÷ 5

$$\begin{array}{r} 7 \\ 5\overline{)369} \end{array}$$

Step 1: Divide. How many 5s are there in 3? (none) How many 5s are there in 36? (7) Place the 7 in the quotient above the 6.

$$\begin{array}{r} 7 \\ 5\overline{)369} \\ -\,35 \\ \hline 1 \end{array}$$

Step 2: Multiply (7 × 5 = 35). Then subtract (36 − 35 = 1). The difference must be less than the divisor (5).

$$\begin{array}{r} 73 \\ 5\overline{)369} \\ -\,35 \\ \hline 19 \\ -\,15 \\ \hline 4 \end{array}$$

Step 3: Bring down the next digit in the dividend. Divide. How many 5s are there in 19? (3) Place the 3 in the quotient above the 9. Multiply (3 × 5 = 15). Subtract (19 − 15 = 4).

$$\begin{array}{r} 73 \text{ R}4 \\ 5\overline{)369} \end{array}$$

Step 4: Write the remainder in the quotient.

The remainder is 4. The four is less than the divisor (5). The remainder must be less than the divisor. The largest possible remainder that any problem could have is always one number less than the divisor.

Look up the word *remainder* in the dictionary. How is *remainder* used in everyday situations? For example: "I spend seven hours in class, and the *remainder* of the day I . . ."

Can you imagine scoring over 10,000 points in 14 years of playing basketball? If a pro basketball player scored 10,318 points by his fourteenth year, how many points would he have averaged per season?

Divide 10318 ÷ 14

Step 1: How many 14s are there in 1? (none)
How many 14s are there in 10? (none)
How many 14s are there in 103? (7)
Place the 7 in the quotient above the three.

$$\begin{array}{r} 7 \\ 14\overline{)10{,}318} \end{array}$$

Step 2: Multiply (7 × 14 = 98). Then subtract (103 − 98 = 5). The difference must be less than the divisor (14).

$$\begin{array}{r} 7 \\ 14\overline{)10{,}318} \\ -\,9\,8 \\ \hline 5 \end{array}$$

Step 3: Bring down the next digit in the dividend. Divide. How many 14s are there in 51? (3) Place the 3 in the quotient above the 1. Multiply (3 × 14 = 42). Subtract (51 − 42 = 9).

$$\begin{array}{r} 73 \\ 14\overline{)10{,}318} \\ -\,9\,8 \\ \hline 51 \\ -\,42 \\ \hline 9 \end{array}$$

Step 4: Bring down the next digit in the dividend. Divide. How many 14s are there in 98? (7) Place the 7 in the quotient above the 8. Multiply (7 × 14 = 98). Subtract (98 − 98 = 0).

The player averaged 737 points per season.

$$\begin{array}{r} 737 \\ 14\overline{)10{,}318} \\ -\,9\,8 \\ \hline 51 \\ -\,42 \\ \hline 98 \\ -\,98 \\ \hline 0 \end{array}$$

quotient — The answer in a division problem.

Dividing a Six-Digit Number by a Three-Digit Number

Divide 349,672 ÷ 436

To divide 349,672 by 436, first look at the 4 in the divisor and the first two digits in the dividend (34). Then divide 34 by 4. The first number in the quotient will probably be 8. Multiply 8 times 436 to determine if 8 is too large (8 × 436 = 3488).

Step 1: How many 436s are there in 349? (none) How many 436s are there in 3496? (8)

$$\begin{array}{r} 8 \\ 436\overline{)349672} \end{array}$$

Step 2: Multiply the quotient by the divisor (8 × 436 = 3488). Subtract (3496 − 3488 = 8). Bring down the next digit in the dividend.

$$\begin{array}{r} 8 \\ 436\overline{)349672} \\ -\ 3488 \\ \hline 87 \end{array}$$

Step 3: Divide. How many 436s are there in 87? (0) Place the zero in the quotient above the 7 in the dividend. Bring down the next digit. How many 436s are there in 872? How many 4s are there in 8? (2) Place the 2 in the quotient above the 2 in the dividend. Multiply (2 × 436 = 872). Subtract (872 − 872 = 0).

$$\begin{array}{r} 802 \\ 436\overline{)349672} \\ -\ 3488 \\ \hline 872 \\ -\ 872 \\ \hline 0 \end{array}$$

349,672 ÷ 436 = 802

Look up the stats of the last five years for your favorite basketball player. How many total points did he or she score for the last five years? Find the average points per year by dividing the total by 5.

Dividing only the first few digits in a division problem is a way of using **estimation**. See pages 44–45 for more details.

Suppose you have 3,763 stamps in a collection. Your school is putting on a hobby fair and they want to display the collection. You go shopping and see different types of display books. Each page of one book can hold approximately 19 stamps. How many pages will you need?

Estimating

In this problem it would be appropriate to find an estimate rather than an exact answer. An estimate is near an exact answer. Nineteen can be rounded to the nearest tens. It is closer to twenty than to ten. The number 3,763 is closer to 4,000 than to 3,000.

Divide 4,000 by 20

Step 1: Divide. How many 20s are there in 40? (2) Multiply (2 × 20 = 40). Subtract (40 − 40 = 0).

$$\begin{array}{r} 2 \\ 20\overline{)4000} \\ -40 \\ \hline 0 \end{array}$$

Step 2: Divide 0 ÷ 20 = 0. Place two zeros in the quotient.

You need approximately 200 pages.

$$\begin{array}{r} 200 \\ 20\overline{)4000} \\ -40 \\ \hline 0 \end{array}$$

I can do this.

Estimating is an important tool when you need to divide two or more digits.

Estimation vs. Finding Exact Quotients

Is the estimated answer in the previous question close to the exact answer? Let's divide 3,763 by 19.

Divide: 3,763 ÷ 19

Step 1: Divide. How many 19s are in 3? (none) How many 19s are there in 37? (one) Multiply (1 × 19 = 19). Subtract (37 − 19 = 18). Bring down the next digit in the dividend (6).

$$
\begin{array}{r}
1 \\
19\overline{)3763} \\
-\ 19 \\
\hline
186
\end{array}
$$

Step 2: Divide. How many 19s are there in 186? (9) Multiply (9 × 19 = 171). Subtract (186 − 171 = 15). Bring down the final digit in the dividend (3).

$$
\begin{array}{r}
19 \\
19\overline{)3763} \\
-19 \\
\hline
186 \\
-\ 171 \\
\hline
153
\end{array}
$$

Step 3: Divide. How many 19s are there in 153? (8) Multiply (8 × 19 = 152). Subtract (153 − 152 = 1). The remainder is one.

The exact answer is 198 R1

$$
\begin{array}{r}
198 \\
19\overline{)3763} \\
-19 \\
\hline
186 \\
-\ 171 \\
\hline
153 \\
-\ 152 \\
\hline
1
\end{array}
$$

You need 199 pages, because 198 pages will be filled and page 199 will have one stamp on it. Your estimation was 200 pages. The estimated quotient is close to the exact answer. An estimated answer can save a lot of time and allow you to check whether the exact answer is reasonable.

Use a calculator to check whether your estimate is close to the exact answer.

Look over the properties of multiplication on page 20. Do they hold true for division?

Commutative Property

Can you change the order when you divide any two numbers and still get the same answer?

Example: Is $10 \div 5$ the same as $5 \div 10$?

Divide. $10 \div 5 = \dfrac{10}{5} = 2$

Divide. $5 \div 10 = \dfrac{5}{10} = \dfrac{1}{2}$

The answers are not the same. Division is not commutative.

Associative Property

Can you change the order when you divide any three or more numbers?

Example: Is $(40 \div 4) \div 2$ the same as $40 \div (4 \div 2)$?

Divide. $(40 \div 4) \div 2$
$$10 \div 2 = 5$$
$$(40 \div 4) \div 2 = 5$$

Divide. $40 \div (4 \div 2)$
$$40 \div 2 = 20$$
$$40 \div (4 \div 2) = 20$$

The answers are not the same. You cannot associate three or more numbers in any way you please when you divide. Division is not associative.

Remember, **parentheses** mean "Do me first."

Distributive Property of Division Over Addition

Does the distributive property hold true for division?

Example: Is 48 ÷ (6 + 2) the same as (48 ÷ 6) + (48 ÷ 2)?

48 ÷ (6 + 2)

Add.

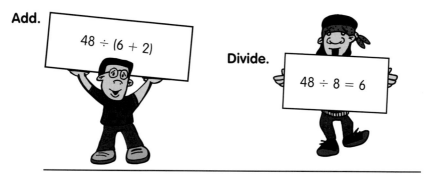

Divide.

(48 ÷ 6) + (48 ÷ 2)

Divide.

Add.

The answers are not the same. The distributive property does not hold true for division.

Suppose at a family picnic, the cook wants to know how many quarter-pound hamburgers can be made from $20\frac{1}{2}$ pounds of ground beef.

It's easier to set up a simpler problem. For example, how many one quarters $\left(\frac{1}{4}\right)$ are there in one whole?

$$\frac{1}{4} + \frac{1}{4} + \frac{1}{4} + \frac{1}{4} = \frac{4}{4} = 1.$$

There are four quarters in one whole.

If there are four quarters in one whole, then how many quarters are there in 20 wholes?

You can make a list to solve this problem:

whole	1	2	3	4	5	6	7	8	9	10
quarters $\left(\frac{1}{4}\right)$	4	8	12	16	20	24	28	32	36	40

whole	11	12	13	14	15	16	17	18	19	20
quarters $\left(\frac{1}{4}\right)$	44	48	52	56	60	64	68	72	76	80

Twenty wholes are the same as 80 quarters.

You could also figure out how many quarters there are in 20 wholes by multiplication:

$$4 \times 20 = 80$$

How many quarters are there in one half? $\left(\frac{1}{2} \text{ is the same as } \frac{2}{4}\right)$ There are two quarters in one half. How many quarter-pound hamburgers can you make if you have $20\frac{1}{2}$ pounds of ground beef? Twenty pounds will give you 80 hamburgers, and a half pound will give you 2. Find the total by adding 80 + 2. You can make 82 hamburgers. That's a big family!

Making a **list** is a strategy that can be used to solve many problems.

Use Pictures to Divide Fractions

Another way to solve this problem is to divide $20\frac{1}{2}$ by $\frac{1}{4}$ using pictures.
How many quarters are there in 1 whole?

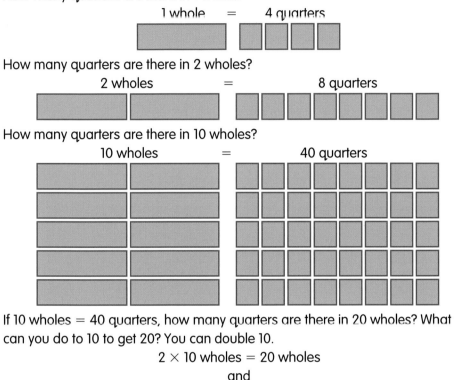

How many quarters are there in 2 wholes?

How many quarters are there in 10 wholes?

If 10 wholes = 40 quarters, how many quarters are there in 20 wholes? What can you do to 10 to get 20? You can double 10.

$$2 \times 10 \text{ wholes} = 20 \text{ wholes}$$
$$\text{and}$$
$$2 \times 40 \text{ quarters} = 80 \text{ quarters}$$

How many quarters are there in $\frac{1}{2}$?

$$\frac{1}{2} = 2 \text{ quarters}$$

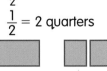

$20\frac{1}{2}$ pounds of ground beef = 82 quarter-pound hamburgers.

Remember: There is more than one way to solve a problem.
When you look at a problem, ask yourself
"What question needs to be answered?" "What facts are given?"

Suppose you are on a one-mile relay team. Each runner runs $\frac{1}{8}$ of a mile. How many runners are on your team? You have to find out how many eighths there are in one whole. Since in a fraction, $\frac{1}{8}$ means 1 out of 8 parts, 8 parts make a whole. There are 8 runners on your team.

Dividing a Fraction by a Fraction

To divide fractions, you need to find the reciprocal of the divisor, then multiply. The reciprocal of a fraction is found by exchanging the numerator for the denominator.

Find the reciprocal of $\frac{1}{8}$

Exchange the numerator and the denominator.

$$\frac{1}{8} \diagdown\!\!\!\!\times\!\!\!\!\diagup \frac{8}{1}$$

The reciprocal of $\frac{1}{8}$ is $\frac{8}{1}$.

Two numbers are reciprocals when their product is 1.

$$\frac{1}{8} \times \frac{8}{1} = \frac{8}{8} = 1.$$

Divide $\frac{3}{4} \div \frac{1}{8}$ (dividend ÷ divisor)

$\frac{1}{8}$ divisor

$\frac{8}{1}$ reciprocal

Step 1: Find the reciprocal of the divisor.

Step 2: Multiply the dividend by the reciprocal of the divisor.

$$\frac{3}{4} \times \frac{8}{1}$$

Step 3: Multiply the numerators. Multiply the denominators.

$$\frac{3 \times 8}{4 \times 1} = \frac{24}{4}$$

Step 4: Reduce to lowest terms.

$$24 \div 4 = 6$$

$$\frac{3}{4} \div \frac{1}{8} = 6$$

Dividing a Whole Number by a Fraction

When dividing a whole number by a fraction, you need to write the whole number as a fraction.

To write a whole number as a fraction, place it over one.

$$\text{For example, } 8 = \frac{8}{1}.$$

It is easier to write a division problem in lowest terms before you solve it.

Example: Reduce $\frac{8}{1} \times \frac{3}{2}$

first factor × second factor

Since 8 is a multiple of 2, you can reduce the numerator of the first factor with the denominator of the second factor.

$$\frac{\overset{4}{\cancel{8}}}{1} \times \frac{3}{\underset{1}{\cancel{2}}} = \frac{12}{1} = 12$$

Divide: $8 \div \frac{2}{3}$

Step 1: Write the whole number as a fraction.

$$\frac{8}{1} \div \frac{2}{3}$$

Step 2: Find the reciprocal of the divisor.

$$\frac{3}{2}$$

Step 3: Multiply the dividend by the reciprocal of the divisor.

$$\frac{8}{1} \times \frac{3}{2} = \frac{24}{2}$$

Step 4: Reduce the answer to lowest terms.

$$\frac{24}{2} = 12$$

A fraction is in lowest terms when the only number that will divide evenly into both the numerator and the denominator is one.

Suppose a printer prints 22 pages in $2\frac{3}{4}$ minutes. How many pages does it print in 1 minute?

Divide $22 \div 2\frac{3}{4}$

To divide a whole number (22) by a mixed number $\left(2\frac{3}{4}\right)$, you must write the mixed number as an improper fraction.

Step 1: Write $2\frac{3}{4}$ as an improper fraction:

Multiply the whole number (2) by the denominator (4).

$$2 \times 4 = 8$$

Add the product (8) to the numerator (3).

$$8 + 3 = 11$$

Write the sum (11) over the denominator (4).

$$2\frac{3}{4} = \frac{11}{4}$$

Step 2: Rewrite the problem.

$$\frac{22}{1} \div \frac{11}{4}$$

Step 3: Find the reciprocal of the divisor.

$$\frac{4}{11}$$

Step 4: Rewrite as a multiplication problem.

$$\frac{22}{1} \times \frac{4}{11}$$

Step 5: Reduce before multiplying.

$$\frac{22 \div 11}{1} \times \frac{4}{11 \div 11}$$

Step 6: Multiply.

$$\frac{2}{1} \times \frac{4}{1} = 8$$

The computer printer can print 8 pages in one minute.

improper fraction — A fraction whose numerator is larger than its denominator.

Dividing Two Mixed Numbers

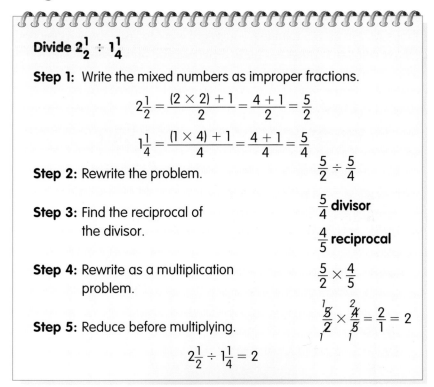

Divide $2\frac{1}{2} \div 1\frac{1}{4}$

Step 1: Write the mixed numbers as improper fractions.

$$2\frac{1}{2} = \frac{(2 \times 2) + 1}{2} = \frac{4 + 1}{2} = \frac{5}{2}$$

$$1\frac{1}{4} = \frac{(1 \times 4) + 1}{4} = \frac{4 + 1}{4} = \frac{5}{4}$$

Step 2: Rewrite the problem.

$$\frac{5}{2} \div \frac{5}{4}$$

Step 3: Find the reciprocal of the divisor.

$\frac{5}{4}$ **divisor**

$\frac{4}{5}$ **reciprocal**

Step 4: Rewrite as a multiplication problem.

$$\frac{5}{2} \times \frac{4}{5}$$

Step 5: Reduce before multiplying.

$$\frac{\overset{1}{\cancel{5}}}{\underset{1}{2}} \times \frac{\overset{2}{\cancel{4}}}{\underset{1}{\cancel{5}}} = \frac{2}{1} = 2$$

$$2\frac{1}{2} \div 1\frac{1}{4} = 2$$

If the **dividend** is less than the **divisor**, the **quotient** will be less than one.

There are many units used to measure time. See the list on page 22 for details.

Sometimes it is necessary to convert units of time. For example, if you rent a video that says it lasts 125 minutes, you might want to know how many hours that is. If it is 4:00 and dinner will be at 6:00, will you have time to watch the whole movie before everyone sits down to eat?

Minutes to Hours

How many hours is 125 minutes? There are 60 minutes in one hour.

Divide 125 minutes by 60 minutes.

Step 1: Divide. How many 60s are there in 125? (2)

$$\frac{2}{60)\overline{125}}$$

Step 2: Multiply (2 × 60 = 120) Subtract (125 − 120 = 5)

$$\begin{array}{r} 2 \\ 60)\overline{125} \\ -\ 120 \\ \hline 5 \end{array}$$

There are 2 hours and 5 minutes in 125 minutes. Your movie will not be over until after 6:00.

Write down the time you go to bed and the time you get up in the morning. How many minutes did you sleep? How many hours?

Months to Years

You just read in the newspaper that a thief was sentenced to 156 months in prison. How many years is 156 months?

One year equals twelve months. When changing time to a larger unit, you use the operation of division. In this problem you need to change months to years.

Divide 156 months ÷ 12 months.

Step 1: Divide ($15 \div 12 = 1$).
Multiply ($1 \times 12 = 12$).

$$12\overline{)156}$$
$$\underline{-\ 12}$$

Step 2: Subtract ($15 - 12 = 3$).
Bring down the 6 in the dividend.

$$12\overline{)156}$$
$$\underline{-\ 12}$$
$$36$$

Step 3: Divide ($36 \div 12 = 3$).
Multiply ($3 \times 12 = 36$).
Subtract ($36 - 36 = 0$).

$$13$$
$$12\overline{)156}$$
$$\underline{-\ 12}$$
$$36$$
$$\underline{-\ 36}$$
$$0$$

There are 13 years in 156 months.

Play Match-Time! Make up pairs of cards that have matching measurements of time (for example, 28 days and 4 weeks). Place the cards facedown. Each player takes a turn and selects two cards. If they match, he keeps the cards and takes another turn. If the cards do not match, he turns them over in the same position. The player with the most matching time cards wins.

dividend — The number being divided.

Decimals are used in measuring time, distance, and money. Division with decimal numbers is almost the same as division with whole numbers. The difference is the placement of the decimal point in the answer.

Dividing a Decimal by a Whole Number

Divide 1.4 ÷ 7

Step 1: Place the decimal point in the quotient directly above the decimal in the dividend.

$$7\overline{)1.4}$$ quotient / dividend

Step 2: Divide. How many 7s are there in 1? (none) Place a zero in the quotient above the 1 in the dividend.

$$7\overline{)1.4} = 0.$$

Step 3: Divide. How many 7s are there in 14? (2) Place the two in the quotient above the four.

$$7\overline{)1.4} = 0.2$$

Step 4: Multiply (2 × 7 = 14). Subtract (14 − 14 = 0). When you subtract, treat the dividend (1.4) as a whole number (14).

$$\begin{array}{r} 0.2 \\ 7\overline{)1.4} \\ -14 \\ \hline 0 \end{array}$$

$$1.4 ÷ 7 = 0.2$$

The zero before the decimal point serves as a placeholder and lets the reader know that there are no ones.

Dividing a Whole Number by a Decimal

To divide by a decimal number, follow these steps.

1. Move the decimal point in the divisor as many places to the right as it takes to make it a whole number.
2. Move the decimal point in the dividend the same number of places as you moved the one in the divisor.
3. Place the decimal point in the quotient directly above the relocated decimal point in the dividend.

Divide 30 ÷ 0.6

$0.6\overline{)30.}$

Step 1: Move the decimal one place to the right in both the divisor (0.6 → 6) and the dividend (30 → 300).

$6\overline{)300}$

Step 2: Divide (30 ÷ 6 = 5). Multiply (5 × 6 = 30).

$$\begin{array}{r} 5 \\ 6\overline{)300} \\ -30 \end{array}$$

Step 3: Subtract (30 − 30 = 0). Divide. How many 6s are in 0? (none)

$$\begin{array}{r} 50 \\ 6\overline{)300} \\ -30 \\ \hline 0 \end{array}$$

$$30 \div 0.6 = 50$$

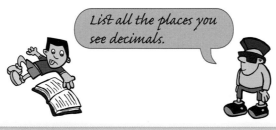

List all the places you see decimals.

A zero to the right of the decimal point, at the end of a number, does not affect its value. For example: 30 = 30.0

Suppose you want to buy one dozen bagels. The individual price for a bagel is 35 cents. Today's special at the bakery is a dozen bagels for $4.08. What is the better buy: the price of an individual bagel or the price per bagel when you buy the special?

$$\text{unit price} = \frac{\text{price}}{\text{quantity}}$$

Let's see what the price per bagel is when you buy the special.

Divide $4.08 by 12

Step 1: Place the decimal point in the quotient.

$$\overset{.\quad\text{quotient}}{12\overline{)4.08}}\ \text{dividend}$$

Step 2: Divide. How many 12s are there in 4? (none) Place the zero in the quotient above the 4 in the dividend. How many 12s are in 40? (3). Place the 3 above the zero in the dividend.

$$\overset{0.3}{12\overline{)4.08}}$$

Step 3: Multiply (3 × 12 = 36). Subtract (40 − 36 = 4).

$$\begin{array}{r}0.3\\12\overline{)4.08}\\-36\\\hline 4\end{array}$$

Step 4: Bring down the next digit in the dividend. How many 12s are in 48? (4) Place the 4 in the quotient above the 8 in the dividend. Subtract (48 − 48 = 0). Write the dollar sign in the quotient.

$$\begin{array}{r}\$0.34\\12\overline{)4.08}\\-36\\\hline 48\\-48\\\hline 0\end{array}$$

One bagel would cost you 34 cents. The regular price for one bagel is 35 cents. The better buy is the bakery special because each bagel would cost you 34 cents instead of 35 cents. (Of course now you have to eat all those bagels.)

Hourly Rate

Your neighbor offers you a baby-sitting job. She offers you $15.30 to baby-sit for five hours. Another neighbor offers you $3.50 per hour to baby-sit for five hours. You can accept only one offer because of your schedule. Which one will pay you the most money?

To find the hourly rate, divide the money amount by the number of hours.

Divide $15.30 ÷ 5

Step 1: Place the decimal point in the quotient.

$$\begin{array}{r} . \quad \text{quotient} \\ 5\overline{)15.30} \quad \text{dividend} \end{array}$$

Step 2: Divide (15 ÷ 5 = 3).
Multiply (3 × 5 = 15).
Subtract (15 − 15 = 0).

$$\begin{array}{r} 3. \\ 5\overline{)15.30} \\ -15 \\ \hline 0 \end{array}$$

Step 3: Bring down the next digit in the dividend. How many 5s are there in 3? (0) Place the zero in the quotient above the 3 in the dividend. Bring down the next digit (0). Divide (30 ÷ 5 = 6). Multiply (6 × 5 = 30). Subtract (30 − 30 = 0). Write the dollar sign in the quotient.

$$\begin{array}{r} \$3.06 \\ 5\overline{)15.30} \\ -15 \\ \hline 30 \\ -30 \\ \hline 0 \end{array}$$

If you baby-sit five hours for $15.30, you will receive $3.06 per hour. It is better to take the hourly rate of $3.50.

Look at a box of your favorite cereal. How much did it cost? How many servings are in the box? How much does your cereal cost per serving?

Remember to place the **decimal point** in the answer and round to the nearest cent.

Sign Combinations

Let's list the different sign combinations.

1. **If you divide two numbers with the same sign, the quotient (answer) is positive.**

   $6 \div 2 = 3$ positive ÷ positive = positive
   $^-6 \div {}^-2 = 3$ negative ÷ negative = positive

2. **If you divide two numbers with unlike signs the quotient (answer) is negative.**

   $^-6 \div 2 = {}^-3$ negative ÷ positive = negative
   $6 \div {}^-2 = {}^-3$ positive ÷ negative = negative

Let's compare the sign combinations of division with those of multiplication.

1. **If you multiply two numbers with the same sign the product (answer) is positive.**

   $6 \times 2 = 12$ positive × positive = positive
   $^-6 \times {}^-2 = 12$ negative × negative = positive

2. **If you multiply two numbers with unlike signs, the product (answer) is negative.**

   $^-6 \times 2 = {}^-12$ negative × positive = negative
   $6 \times {}^-2 = {}^-12$ positive × negative = negative

Since multiplication and division are inverse operations, the sign combinations are the same. If you multiply or divide two integers with the same sign, the answer will be positive. If you multiply or divide two integers with unlike signs, the answer will be negative.

inverse operations:
   Addition is the inverse of subtraction.
   Multiplication is the inverse of division.

Meteorologists divide integers to find average temperatures.
Suppose a meteorologist recorded the following temperatures for one week:

$$5° F, \quad {}^-4° F, \quad 0° F, \quad {}^-3° F, \quad 1° F, \quad {}^-8° F, \quad 2° F$$

To find the average temperature for the week, add the temperatures. Then divide by the total number of days.

Find the average temperature.

Step 1: Add the integers two at a time. Take the sign of 5 (+). $5 + {}^-4 = 1$

Step 2: Add the sum to the next integer. $1 + 0 = 1$

Step 3: Add the sum in step 2 to the next integer. Take the sign of 3 ($^-$). $1 + {}^-3 = {}^-2$

Step 4: Add the sum in step 3 to the next integer. Take the sign of 2 ($^-$). ${}^-2 + 1 = {}^-1$

Step 5: Add the sum in step 4 to the next integer. ${}^-1 + {}^-8 = {}^-9$

Step 6: Add the sum in step 5 to the next integer. ${}^-9 + 2 = {}^-7$

Step 7: Divide the sum by the total number of days (7). ${}^-7 \div 7 = {}^-1$

The average temperature was $^-1°$ F. The average does not have to be one of the temperatures. It represents the group. The average is always somewhere between the lowest and highest number in a group.

Follow a particular stock for seven days. What was the average fluctuation?

When adding integers with unlike signs (positive and negative) subtract the two integers and take the sign of the number that is larger. If the integers have the same sign add the two and keep the sign.

Further Reading

Books

Hood, Christine. *Practice! Practice! Practice! Multiplication & Division: 50 Independent Practice Pages That Help Kids Master Essential Math Skills-and Meet the NCTM Standards.* New York: Teaching Resources, 2005.

McMullen, Chris. *Practice Adding, Subtracting, Multiplying and Dividing Fractions Workbook: Improve Your Math Fluency Series.* New York: CreateSpace, 2010.

Zegarelli, Mark. *Basic Math and Pre Algebra Workbook for Dummies.* New Jersey: Wiley Publishing Inc., 2008.

Internet Addresses

Aplusmath.com: *Flashcards.* © 2000. <http://www.aplusmath.com/Flashcards/index.html>.

Math2.org. <http://www.math2.org/index.html>.

The Math Forum. *Ask Dr. Math.* © 1994–2004. <http://mathforum.org/dr.math/>.

Mrs. Glosser's Math Goodies, Inc. *Mrs. Glosser's Math Goodies.* © 1999–2000. <http://www.mathgoodies.com>.

A
associative property, 20, 46

C
checking the answer, 13
closure property, 20
commutative property, 20, 46

D
decimals, 24–25, 26, 56–57
distributive property of division
    over addition, 47
distributive property of multiplication
    over addition, 21
division
    of decimals, 56–57
    and estimation, 44–45
    facts, 32–33, 35
    of fractions, 49, 50–51
    of greater numbers, 42–43
    of integers, 60–61
    of mixed numbers, 52–53
    of money, 58–59
    by multiples of ten, 38–39
    and multiplication, 34–37
    and problem solving, 48–49
    properties, 46–47
    terms, 37
    of time, 54

E
estimation, 16–17, 44–45

F
fractions, 28–29, 50–51

G
greater numbers, 14–15, 42–43

I
integers, 30–31, 60–61
inverse operations, 34, 35, 36

L
lattice multiplication, 19

M
mixed numbers, 29, 52
money, 26–27, 58–59
multiples of ten, 10–11,
    38–39
multiplication
    and addition, 6–7
    of decimals, 24–25
    and division, 34–37
    and estimation, 16–17
    facts, 8–9
    of fractions, 28–29
    of greater numbers, 14–15
    of integers, 30–31
    methods, 18–19
    of money, 26–27
    by multiples of ten, 10–11
    properties, 20–21
    and regrouping, 12–13
    table, 8
    of time, 22–23

N
number sentences, 6–7

P
partial products, 13
place value, 12, 15
powers of ten, 27, 39
property of one, 21

R

regrouping, 12–13

remainders, 40–41

repeated addition, 6, 12, 31

rounding, 16, 17, 27

Russian peasant method of
multiplication, 18

S

sign combinations, 60

T

time, 22–23, 54–55

W

whole numbers, 24, 25, 26, 34, 51,
56, 57

Z

zero property, 21